The Most Amazing Rice Cooker Recipes

The Innovative Rice Cooker Meals for you all 24/7

Table of Contents

Introduction 4

1. Carrot Parsnip Puree 6
2. Vegetables with Garlic Baguette 8
3. Coconut Butternut Squash 11
4. Chickpea Vegetable Pilaf 13
5. Baked Haricot Beans 16
6. Sausage and Chestnut Mushrooms 18
7. Couscous Pearls with Tomatoes 21
8. Braised olive and Fennel 24
9. Mixed Vegetables on Bed of Rice 26
10. Stuffed Red Bell Peppers 29
11. Fennel Couscous with Kalamata Olives and Chickpeas 31
12. Tempeh Curry 33
13. Braised Fennel 36
14. Risotto with Peas 38
15. Tofu in Mushroom Onion Gravy 41
16. Fruits and Vegetable Stew 44
17. Rice Cooker-Fried Brussel Sprouts with Roasted Peanuts 46
18. Quick and Easy Vegetable Curry 48

19. Spicy Red Lentils 51

20. Loin Pork in Orange Sauce 54

21. Cheesy Spinach Lasagna 56

22. Beef Bourguignon 59

23. Lentil Curry 62

24. Braised Sweet Onions in Olive Oil and Vinegar 64

25. Tuna Steaks in Olive Oil 66

26. Chicken Breasts with Yogurt and Beer 68

27. Baked Onions and Tomatoes 70

28. Stewed Green and Red Cabbage 73

29. Vegetable Chili and Zucchini 76

30. Christmas Pumpkin and Red Bean Curry 79

Introduction

Cooking rice in a rice cooker is something that everyone is conversant with. When we crave fluffy, well cooked, and soft rice grains, we know how to make it with our rice cooker.

But that is not all the magic that you can create with your rice cooker. Cooking rice every day with your rice cooker is cool stuff, but do you crave to take things a step further?

Do you want to learn unimaginable ways that you can cook other things with your rice cooker?

If your answer is a resounding yes, then purchasing this cookbook is the best thing that can ever happen to you!

This rice cooker recipe book that is not entirely a rice cooker recipe book is here to take your cooking a step higher. And I am here to help you on this journey!

So, put your seat belt on, grab this recipe book and allow your rice cooker to take you on a trip!!!

1. Carrot Parsnip Puree

Serves: 4

Time: 20 mins.

The list of ingredients:

- 2 tbsp. extra virgin olive oil
- 4 cups parsnips
- 1 tsp. coconut sugar
- A pinch of pepper
- 1/4 cup vegetable stock

- 2 cups, thinly sliced carrots
- 1 tsp. ground cumin
- A pinch of salt

Method:

Step 1

Combine the cumin, parsnips, carrots, oil, coconut sugar, salt, pepper, and vegetable stock in a rice cooker. Cover using lid and cook for approximately 10 minutes.

Step 2

Puree mixture in a blender until becomes smooth.

Step 3

Serve immediately.

2. Vegetables with Garlic Baguette

Serves: 4

Time: 30 mins.

The list of ingredients:

- 1 red, chunked bell pepper
- 2 tbsp. plain flour
- 1 vegetarian baguette
- 1 yellow, chunked bell pepper
- 4 crushed garlic cloves

- 2/3 cup pitted, black olives
- 1 can tomatoes
- 1 small, chunked eggplant
- 2 chunked courgettis
- chopped Parsley leaves
- a pinch of pepper
- 2 tbsp. olive oil
- 1 cup vegetable stock
- a pinch of salt
- 1 chopped onion
- 2 tbsp. pesto

Method:

Step 1

Toss the eggplant, onion, and the bell peppers for approximately 5 minutes.

Step 2

Heat the olive oil in a rice cooker and toss the eggplant, onion, and bell peppers for roughly 5 minutes.

Step 3

Add the garlic and courgettes then cook for a minimum of 3 minutes.

Step 4

Pour over the flour, tomatoes, and vegetable stock then bring mixture to a boil. Cook for roughly 10 minutes.

Step 5

Stir in the pesto and olives into the vegetables. Season using salt and pepper then serve the veggies with the garlic baguette.

3. Coconut Butternut Squash

Serves: 4

Time: 15 mins.

The list of ingredients:

- 1/2 cup vegetable stock
- 1 tbsp. extra-virgin olive oil
- 1 tsp. coconut sugar
- 6 cups butternut squash
- 1 tbsp. thyme leaves

- 3 tbsp. coconut milk
- A pinch of pepper
- 1 finely chopped onion
- A pinch of salt

Method:

Step 1

In the rice cooker, heat the oil then stir in the onions. Put the squash (butternut) in the rice cooker. Cook for approximately 5 minutes. Add the salt, pepper, coconut sugar.

Step 2

Stir mixture for roughly 1 minute then add vegetable stock and cook for an additional 5 minutes.

Step 3

Use a spoon to mash the squash and stir in the coconut milk with the thyme. Serve hot. Enjoy.

4. Chickpea Vegetable Pilaf

Serves: 4

Time: 25 mins.

The list of ingredients:

- 3 tbsp. olive oil
- A pinch of pepper
- wedges lime
- 2 bay leaves
- 1 large, finely chopped onion

- large pinch saffron threads
- 2 tsp. ginger
- 1 tbsp. tomato puree
- 2 cardamom pods
- 1 medium, cubed eggplant
- 4 cups vegetable stock
- 1 stick cinnamon
- 3 oz. dried apricots
- A pinch of salt
- handful coriander
- 2 tsp. minced garlic
- 1 cup raisins
- 1 can chickpeas
- 5 oz. cherry tomatoes
- 1 cup brown rice

Method:

Step 1

In a rice cooker heat 1 tbsp of oil. For 3 minutes stir in the onions thoroughly. Put in the remaining oil with the garlic, cinnamon stick, eggplant, bay leaves and cardamom. For 5 minutes, sauté.

Step 2

Put in the saffron and stock. Stir in the apricots, tomato puree, brown rice, raisins, chickpeas, and cherry tomatoes. Heat till mixture boils.

Step 3

Transfer to the rice cooker. Use the lid to cover and cook for approximately 12 minutes. Remove the cinnamon stick and use salt and pepper to season. Use fresh coriander with lime and wedges to sprinkle.

5. Baked Haricot Beans

Serves: 4

Time: 35 mins.

The list of ingredients:

- 2 cups passata
- 4 tbsp. tomato puree
- 2 chopped onions
- 2 tsp. mustard powder
- 1/2 cup brown sugar

- 1 finely diced carrot
- 2 cups dried, soaked in cold water haricot beans
- 1 bay leaf
- 2 sticks finely diced celery sticks
- a pinch of salt

Method:

Step 1

First step is to place the beans (soaked) in a rice cooker.

Step 2

Next press the 'cook' button on the rice cooker then cook for approximately 10 minutes. Drain. Set aside.

Step 3

Add in the carrot, onions, and celery sticks, mustard powder, brown sugar, salt, bay leaf, tomato puree and passata then bring to a boil.

Step 4

Pour bean mixture into the rice cooker then using the lid cover rice cooker and cook for 12-15 minutes on low until beans becomes tender. Enjoy.

6. Sausage and Chestnut Mushrooms

Serves: 5

Time: 25 mins.

The list of ingredients:

- 1 cut into chunks courgettes
- 1 tbsp. chopped sage
- 2 tbsp. plain flour
- 1 cup shredded cabbage
- 1 tbsp. mustard

- a pinch of pepper
- 1 pack chestnuts
- 2 ½ cups vegetable stock
- 1 tbsp. olive oil
- 1 large, cut into chunks carrots
- a pinch of salt
- 5 cut into 3 pieces quorn sausages
- 1 lb. chestnut mushrooms
- 1 large, chopped onion

Method:

Step 1

Press the 'cook' button on the rice cooker.

Step 2

Heat oil then cook sausages for approximately 5 minutes. Add in mushrooms and carrots. Stir thoroughly for 4 minutes.

Step 3

Sprinkle flour along with the sage. Stir until all ingredients are well coated by the flour. Put the stock and bring to boil. Stir the mustard with the chestnuts.

Step 4

Put mixture into the rice cooker and add the courgette cover and cook for approximately 7 minutes.

Step 5

Add cabbage and let simmer for 5 approximately minutes. Serve and enjoy.

7. Couscous Pearls with Tomatoes

Serves: 4

Time: 25 mins.

The list of ingredients:

- 1/8 tsp. white pepper
- 1 lb. cubed, firm tomatoes
- 1/2 tsp. sweet paprika powder
- 1 tbsp. minced garlic
- 1/16 tsp. turmeric powder

- 1/16 tsp. cumin powder
- 1 cup vegetable stock
- 1/4 tsp. kosher salt
- red chili flakes
- 1/16 tsp. cardamom powder
- 1/16 tsp. cinnamon powder
- 2 cups couscous pearls
- 1 cup water
- 1/16 tsp. coriander powder
- 3 tbsp. olive oil
- 1/2 cup minced onions
- 1/4 cup freshly squeezed lemon juice
- 1/16 tsp. ginger powder

Method:

Step 1

On the rice cooker press the 'cook' button. Heat the oil. Sauté onion and garlic for 2 minutes. Add and combine cardamom powder, turmeric powder, couscous pearls, vegetable stock, water, red chili flakes, ginger powder, sweet paprika powder, cumin powder, coriander powder, cardamom powder, turmeric powder, cinnamon powder, salt, and pepper.

Step 2

Using the lid cover and cook for 15 minutes or when the couscous is cooked. Squeeze juice out of the lemon. Adjust taste to your liking.

Step 3

Ladle into plates and serve. Use fresh tomatoes to garnish.

8. Braised olive and Fennel

Serves: 6

Time: 20 mins.

The list of ingredients:

- 4 medium fennel bulbs
- 2 tbsp. sugar
- 1 grated lemon grind
- 12 black olives
- crusty wheat bread

- 1 can chopped tomatoes
- 1 tbsp. olive oil
- 1/2 cup vegetarian, parmesan cheese
- 1 juice lemon
- 2 tbsp. tomato puree

Method:

Step 1

Ensure that fennel is trimmed then take away any discolored parts from the base of funnel.

Step 2

Thinly slice then toss in the lemon juice and scatter into the base of rice cooker.

Step 3

Add in the olive oil, lemon rind, tomatoes, tomato puree, olives and sugar.

Step 4

Cover using the lid and cook for approximately 10 minutes.

Step 5

Scatter using the vegetarian parmesan and let melt. Serve with wheat bread.

9. Mixed Vegetables on Bed of Rice

Serves: 4

Time: 25 mins.

The list of ingredients:

- a pinch of pepper
- 2 tbsp. maple syrup
- 2 tsp. minced ginger
- 1 tsp. ground turmeric
- 1 large courgettes

- 1 cup baby spinach
- 1 can chickpeas
- brown rice
- 2 cups butternut, chunked squash
- 1 can chopped tomatoes
- 1 tbsp. harissa paste
- 2 tsp. minced garlic
- a pinch of salt
- 1 large, wedged onion
- handful fresh mint
- 1 ¼ cups vegetable stock
- handful coriander
- 2 diced carrots
- 1 large diced red bell pepper
- 2 tbsp. olive oil

Method:

Step 1

In a rice cooker, begin to heat the oil and add the onion.

Step 2

Sauté for approximately 5 minutes then add the butternut squash and carrots then stir for approximately 5 minutes.

Step 3

Stir in the courgettes, garlic, ginger, harissa, turmeric, tomatoes, bell pepper and the vegetable stock.

Step 4

Season using salt and pepper and bring mixture to a boil. Place mixture into the rice cooker then cover the rice cooker using the lid. Cook for roughly 5 minutes.

Step 5

Stir in the spinach, chickpeas, maple syrup, and ½ of the mint and coriander. Serve on top of the brown rice.

10. Stuffed Red Bell Peppers

Serves: 4

Time: 20 mins.

The list of ingredients:

- 2 diced celeries
- 1 cup herb stuffing mix
- 1 tbsp. olive oil
- a pinch of salt
- 4 red, cored bell peppers

- 2 plum tomatoes

Method:

Step 1   Mix 3/4 cup of water and oil in a bowl (microwavable). Microwave for a minute. Put the stuffing mix in the bowl and microwave for a next 2 minutes. Stir thoroughly.

Step 2   In a medium-sized bowl, combine the celery and the tomatoes. Stir thoroughly. Add salt. Stir to combine.

Step 3   Distribute the stuffing/mixture equally among 4 peppers. Put into the rice cooker. Pour the boiling water until it comes halfway up. Press the 'cook' button and cook for approximately 12 minutes.

Step 4   Serve. Enjoy.

11. Fennel Couscous with Kalamata Olives and Chickpeas

Serves: 4

Time: 15 mins.

The list of ingredients:

- 1/2 small, thinly sliced fennel bulb
- 2 cups not instant couscous pearls
- a pinch of salt
- 1 tbsp. olive oil

- 1/4 cup freshly squeezed lemon juice
- 1 cup mushroom stock
- 1/2 cup black pitted, in brine Kalamata olives
- 1 cup water
- 1 can rinsed, drained chickpeas

Method:

Step 1

First step is to press the cook button on the rice cooker and begin to heat the oil.

Step 2

Sauté the fennel bulb for approximately 3 minutes until it is seared brown.

Step 3

Add in the Kalamata olives, chickpeas, couscous, water,

Step 4

mushroom stock and salt.

Step 5

Close the rice cooker using the lid and cook for roughly 5 minutes.

Step 6

When finished, squeeze the lemon juice then adjust taste if needed. Serve.

12. Tempeh Curry

Serves: 4

Time: 15 mins.

The list of ingredients:

- chopped cilantro
- 2 black, crushed cardamom pods
- 2 tbsp. extra virgin olive oil
- 2 tsp ground coriander
- 1 stick cinnamon

- 1 tsp. ground cumin
- 1 cup coconut milk
- 3 cloves minced coriander
- 2 long, red, minced chilis
- 2 finely chopped onions
- 1 tsp. Dijon mustard
- 2 cups tempeh
- a pinch of pepper
- 2 tbsp. minced gingerroot
- a pinch of salt
- 1 cup vegetable stock
- 1 tsp. ground turmeric

Method:

Step 1

In a rice cooker, heat the oil. Add the tempeh and stir until light brown.

Step 2

Add the remaining oil and cook the onions for 4 minutes. Put in the garlic, pepper, cumin, coriander, turmeric, gingerroot, salt, cardamom pods, cinnamon stick and cook for 1 minute. Add the stock to the mixture and heat mixture till it boils.

Step 3

Use the lid to cover and cook for 5 minutes.

Step 4

In a bowl (small), mix the mustard, chilis and coconut milk. Stir into the tempeh. Use the lid to cover and cook for another 2 minutes. Use cilantro to garnish.

13. Braised Fennel

Serves: 6

Time: 15 mins.

The list of ingredients:

- 2 tbsp. extra virgin olive oil
- A pinch of pepper
- 3 minced garlic cloves
- 1 thinly sliced onion
- Fennel fronds

- 4 fennels, thinly sliced Bulbs
- A pinch of salt
- 1 can diced tomatoes with juice

Method:

Step 1

Press the 'cook' button and then heat the oil. Add the fennel bulbs and onion. Toss and cook for 5 minutes.

Step 2

Add the garlic, salt, and pepper. Continue stirring for an additional minute. Add the tomatoes with juice and then boil.

Step 3

Use the lid to cover and cook for an additional 3 minutes. Garnish with fennel fronds.

14. Risotto with Peas

Serves: 4

Time: 50 mins.

The list of ingredients:

- vegetarian, parmesan cheese
- 5 cups vegetable stock
- a pinch of pepper
- lemon juice
- 1 crushed garlic clove

- a pinch of salt
- 1 ½ cup vegan risotto rice
- 2 cups finely chopped fennel bulbs
- 2 tbsp. olive oil
- 1 cup frozen peas
- finely grated lemon rind

Method:

Step 1

In a rice cooker, begin to heat the olive oil then fry the fennel bulbs and garlic.

Step 2

Next, stir in the lemon rind and juice for approximately 5 minutes.

Step 3

Occasionally stir, until fennel begins to soften.

Step 4

Pour in the risotto and the vegetable stock then bring mixture to a boil.

Step 5

Transfer all contents to the rice cooker and cover then cook for 5 minutes.

Step 6

Stir in the peas then let simmer for an additional 30 minutes.

Step 7

Season using salt and pepper and serve with the Parmesan cheese (scattered).

15. Tofu in Mushroom Onion Gravy

Serves: 4

Time: 45 mins.

The list of ingredients:

- 2 minced garlic cloves
- 1 cup water
- 1 tbsp. tomato paste
- 3 thinly sliced onions
- 2 tbsp. olive oil

- 1 tsp. dried thyme
- 1 pack, firm tofu
- 8 oz. cremini, sliced mushrooms
- a pinch of pepper
- 1 package dried porcini mushrooms
- a pinch of salt
- 1/2 cup dry sherry
- 1 bay leaf

Method:

Step 1

Prepare from before: In a medium-sized bowl, combine water and mushrooms. Let it sit for approximately half an hour.

Step 2

Using a paper towel dry the mushrooms by patting and chop. Put aside the liquid and mushroom

Step 3

In a rice cooker, heat oil and add tofu. Stir for 4 minutes. Add the garlic, bay leaf, onions, garlic, thyme, salt, pepper, and the reserved mushrooms. Stir in tomato paste thoroughly. Put in the sherry and the retained liquid. Heat until it boils.

Step 4

Stir in the mushrooms thoroughly. Use the lid to cover and cook for approximately 10 minutes. Remove the bay leaf.

16. Fruits and Vegetable Stew

Serves: 3

Time: 20 mins.

The list of ingredients:

- 1 can chopped tomatoes
- brown rice
- 1 cup dried, quartered apricots
- 2 tsp. minced ginger
- 1 cup green, trimmed beans

- 2 fat, deseeded red chilies
- 1 tsp. ground Turmeric
- 2/3 cup vegetable stock
- 1 tsp. ground Coriander
- 2 cups roasted cashew nuts
- 1 large, red, chunked pepper
- 2 tbsp. olive oil
- 1 tsp. ground cumin
- 2 tsp. minced garlic
- 2 tbsp. mango chutney

Method:

Step 1

Press the 'cook' button on the rice cooker. Heat the oil then stir in garlic, ginger, chilies, and red pepper. Stir thoroughly and cook for approximately 2 minutes.

Step 2

Add in ground spices, tomatoes, stock, apricots, mango chutney and beans. Cook for approximately 10 minutes.

Step 3

Scatter the nuts (cashew) on the stew and serve with brown rice.

17. Rice Cooker-Fried Brussel Sprouts with Roasted Peanuts

Serves: 4

Time: 25 mins.

The list of ingredients:

- 1/4 tsp. fresh lemon zest
- 1/2 tbsp. peanut oil
- 1/8 cup water
- 2 cups bottoms trimmed Brussels sprouts

- 1/4 cup lightly salted, roasted peanuts
- 1/8 tsp. salt
- 3 tbsp. freshly squeezed lemon juice
- 2 cups white, cooked rice
- 1/2 tbsp. palm sugar
- 1/8 tsp. black pepper

Method:

Step 1

First step is to press the cook button on the rice cooker and mix together the white rice (cooked), peanut oil, brussels sprouts, lemon zest, sugar, black pepper, and water. Cook for approximately 5 minutes.

Step 2

When finished, remove the lid from the rice cooker. Adjust taste if needed. Serve.

Step 3

Squeeze in the lemon juice and sprinkle the roasted peanuts.

Step 4

Serve with the rice (steamed) or bread.

18. Quick and Easy Vegetable Curry

Serves: 4

Time: 20 mins.

The list of ingredients:

- 1/2 cup cubed carrot
- 1 cup cubed squash
- 1/4 tsp. cinnamon powder
- 1/4 tsp. red pepper flakes
- 1/4 tsp. cumin powder

- 1 tbsp. tomato paste
- 1 tbsp. grated ginger
- 1/8 tsp. turmeric powder
- 1 cup cubed potato
- 1 tbsp. curry powder
- 1/8 tsp. black pepper
- 1/8 tsp. coriander powder
- 1 cup minced onion
- 1/2 cup red bell pepper
- 1-piece halved banana chili
- 1/4 tsp. salt
- 1 tbsp. olive oil
- 2 tbsp. minced garlic
- 1 can whole button, quartered mushrooms
- 2 cups vegetable broth
- 1/2 tsp. Spanish paprika
- 1 cup water
- 1 tbsp. brown sugar
- 2 cups brown, cooked rice
- 1/2 cup cubed sweet potato
- 2 cans thick, divided coconut cream

For garnish: 2 tbsp. fresh alfalfa sprouts

Method:

Step 1

Mix together curry powder, brown sugar, cumin powder, Spanish paprika, cinnamon powder, turmeric powder, coriander powder, red pepper flakes, salt, and pepper, in a bowl. Mix then set aside.

Step 2

First step is to press the "cook" button on the rice cooker then you heat the oil. Sauté onion, garlic, and ginger until translucent and gives of a scent. Add the spices. Cook for approximately 3 minutes.

Step 3

Add in squash, vegetable broth, tomato paste, water, and brown rice, potato, carrot, sweet potato, red bell pepper, whole button mushrooms, banana, chili. Cook for approximately 10 minutes.

Step 4

Add coconut cream. Adjust seasoning to your taste.

Step 5

Serve ladled into bowls. Use alfalfa sprouts to garnish.

19. Spicy Red Lentils

Serves: 6

Time: 20 mins.

The list of ingredients:

- 1/4 tsp. cayenne powder
- 1/4 tsp. red chili flakes
- 1 tsp. salt
- 2 tsp. coriander powder
- 2 tbsp. olive oil

- 1/2 tsp. cinnamon powder
- 1/4 tsp. nutmeg powder
- 4 tbsp. freshly squeezed lemon juice
- 1/8 cup diced red bell pepper
- 2 cups vegetable stock
- 1 ½ cup red lentils
- 1/4 tsp. clove powder
- 1/2 cup minced onion
- 6 cups water
- 4 cups torn, packed, fresh kale leaves
- 1/2 tsp. turmeric powder
- 1/8 inch black pepper
- 1/4 tsp. cardamom powder
- 1 tsp. garlic powder

Method:

Step 1

First step is to press the cook button on the rice cooker and begin to heat the olive oil.

Step 2

Sauté the onion for approximately 2 minutes and add in the garlic powder, lentils, clove powder, coriander powder, red chili flakes, cardamom powder, cinnamon powder, cayenne powder, turmeric powder, and nutmeg powder. Stir well.

Step 3

Pour the water and vegetable stock then add in the bell pepper. Season using salt and pepper. Cook for an additional 10 minutes. Serve.

20. Loin Pork in Orange Sauce

Serves: 4

Time: 25 mins.

The list of ingredients:

- 2 cups boneless, cubed pork tenderloin
- 1 tsp. salt
- 3 tbsp. olive oil
- 1/4 tsp. ground black pepper
- 1 thinly sliced onion

- 2 tbsp. freshly squeezed lime juice
- 1 crumbled bay leaf
- 3 minced garlic cloves
- 3/4 cups freshly squeezed orange juice
- 1 tsp. ground cumin
- 1 sliced into wedges lemon
- 1 tsp. dried oregano

Method:

Step 1

Press the "cook" button. Brown the pork tenderloin for 5 minutes on all sides. Set aside.

Step 2

Sauté the onion and garlic for 3 minutes or until translucent and aromatic. Add the lime and orange juices, bay leaf, dried oregano, ground cumin, salt, and pepper. Add the browned pork and its juices.

Step 3

Cook for 12 minutes. When done cooking, adjust taste as needed.

Step 4

Serve with lemon wedges.

21. Cheesy Spinach Lasagna

Serves: 4

Time: 15 mins.

The list of ingredients:

- 8 oz. baby leaf spinach
- grated nutmeg
- Lasagna sheets
- grated mozzarella cheese
- a pinch of salt

- 1 cup soft goat's cheese
- a pinch of pepper

Method:

Step 1

Gradually rinse the spinach under running water (cold) then drain.

Step 2

Place the spinach (drained) into a saucepan then heats until it becomes wilted. Drain well.

Step 3

Place the spinach in a bowl then stir in the cheese.

Step 4

Season using salt, nutmeg and pepper then spread into the Lasagna sheets and tightly roll up.

Step 5

Pour 1/2 of tomato sauce into rice cooker then evenly arrange cannelloni over the sauce. Pour in the remaining sauce.

Step 6

Hit the 'cook' button on the rice cooker then cook for approximately 10 minutes.

Step 7

Sprinkle over the mozzarella cheese then serve using salad leaves.

22. Beef Bourguignon

Serves: 8

Time: 15 mins.

The list of ingredients:

- 1/2 tsp. dried rosemary
- 2 lbs., boneless, cut into cubes beef chunk
- 3 cups dry red wine
- 1 tsp. salt
- 1/2 tsp. black pepper

- 1/2 cup chopped carrots
- 1 tbsp. minced parsley
- 3 tbsp. all-purpose flour
- 3 tbsp. olive oil
- 1/2 tsp. dried thyme
- 1/4 tsp. ground black pepper
- 2 minced garlic cloves
- 1 cup white button, trimmed mushrooms
- 1/2 cup peeled onions

Method:

Step 1

Prepare before: Using a bowl (nonreactive), combine beef chunks, dry red wine, garlic, salt, pepper, thyme, and rosemary. Cover and refrigerate for roughly 3 hours or overnight.

Step 2

Discard of the marinated beef and dry by patting. keep the marinade liquids.

Step 3

Meanwhile, in a bowl, put together flour, salt, and pepper. Dredge the marinated beef into the mixture.

Step 4

Press the 'cook' button on the rice cooker.

Step 5

Heat olive oil, once hot, let the carrots sauté for 3 minutes. Add the onions. Sauté for approximately 2 minutes. Add the browned meat, the mushrooms, and the marinade retained. Cook for approximately 20 minutes.

Step 6

Adjust taste of needed. Serve by sprinkling parsley.

23. Lentil Curry

Serves: 2

Time: 25 mins.

The list of ingredients:

- 1/2 tsp. ground cumin
- 2 ½ cups vegetable stocks
- 1/2 tsp. minced ginger
- 1 can chopped tomatoes
- 1/2 tsp. minced garlic

- 1 tbsp. olive oil
- 1 cup baby spinach
- handful curry leaves
- 1/2 tsp. ground coriander
- 1 large, finely chopped onion
- 1 cup red lentils

Method:

Step 1

Under running water (cold), rinse the lentils.

Step 2

When finished, drain then place into the rice cooker. Cook for approximately 10 minutes then set aside.

Step 3

Heat the olive oil into the rice cooker then adds the onion and curry leaves. Stir mixture for 3 minutes and add the ginger, ground ingredient and garlic. Stir for roughly 5 minutes.

Step 4

Add the tomatoes and stocks then bring mixture to a boil.

Step 5

Pour mixture over the lentils then cover rice cooker and cook for 3 minutes.

24. Braised Sweet Onions in Olive Oil and Vinegar

Serves: 10

Time: 15 mins.

The list of ingredients:

- 6 quartered sweet onions
- 2 tbsp. balsamic vinegar
- A pinch of pepper
- finely chopped parsley

- 3 tbsp. extra virgin olive oil
- A pinch of salt

Method:

Step 1

Combine the olive oil, vinegar, onions, salt, and pepper in a rice cooker and toss until thoroughly combined. Sprinkle using more olive oil.

Step 2

Cover lid and cook for approximately 3-5 minutes on low garnish using parsley.

25. Tuna Steaks in Olive Oil

Serves: 4

Time: 30 mins. + Marinating time

The list of ingredients:

- a pinch of hot pepper flakes
- 2 tbsp. coarsely chopped parsley
- 2 cut into 1 inch thick tuna steaks
- 3 crumbled bay leaves
- 2 tsp. salt

- 2/3 cup extra virgin olive
- 2 cups water
- 2 crushed garlic cloves

Method:

Step 1

In a bowl (large), combine the olive oil, bay leaves, garlic, salt, and pepper then put aside.

Step 2

Pour water inside of the rice cooker then grease the steaming basket with the olive oil. Layer tuna steaks without overlapping the. Place steamer basket on the rice cooker.

Step 3

Press 'cook' button and cook for approximately 12 minutes.

Step 4

Open the lid then Carefully remove the steamer basket. Place tuna steaks in a large platter. use the marinade to pour over the tuna. Allow the tuna to marinate for approximately 120 minutes at room temperature. For 2-4 hours.

Step 5

Sprinkle parsley to serve.

26. Chicken Breasts with Yogurt and Beer

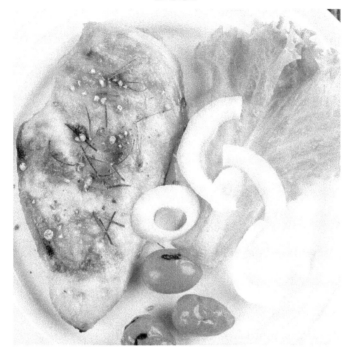

Serves: 4

Time: 15 mins.

The list of ingredients:

- 1/2 tsp. salt
- 1/2 tsp. oregano
- 1/2 tsp. paprika
- 1/4 tsp. ground black pepper

- 4 halved chicken breasts
- 1/2 cup beer
- 1 thinly sliced onion
- 1 cup plain yogurt
- 3 tbsp. olive oil

Method:

Step 1

First step is to press the cook button on the rice cooker and begin to heat the olive oil.

Step 2

Once the olive oil becomes hot begin to add the chicken breasts and cook for approximately 4 minutes on both sides then set aside.

Step 3

Sauté the onion for roughly 3 minutes and ensure that chicken breasts are not browned.

Step 4

Gradually stir in the oregano, paprika, salt, and pepper then add in the beer and yogurt.

Step 5

Cook for an additional 10 minutes and adjust taste if needed. Serve.

27. Baked Onions and Tomatoes

Serves: 6

Time: 30 mins.

The list of ingredients:

- 1 crushed garlic clove
- 1/2 cup dried breadcrumbs
- 2 large onions
- 2/3 cup vegetable stock

- 2 tbsp. sun-dried tomato paste
- a pinch salt
- 6 sun-blushed in oil tomatoes
- a pinch of pepper
- 4 large, shredded basil

Method:

Step 1

Bring a pan to a boil and add the onions (whole) while they are in their skins. Boil for approximately 10 minutes then drain and set aside to cool.

Step 2

Once the onions have cooled begin to peel the onions then gradually slice them in half horizontally.

Step 3

Scoop the center of the onion leaving at least a shell of 3 layers. Chop the scooped-out onions and place in a bowl.

Step 4

Add in the tomato paste, breadcrumbs, garlic, tomatoes (sun-blushed), basil, salt, and pepper.

Step 5

Spoon stuffing into onions and place into the rice cooker. Pour stock around the onions and cook for approximately 8-10 minutes then serve.

28. Stewed Green and Red Cabbage

Serves: 8

Time: 15 mins.

The list of ingredients:

- 1/4 cup loosely packed fresh, roughly torn parsley tops
- 1/2 tsp. red pepper flakes
- 1 cup water
- 1/2 tsp. kosher salt

- 1/4 cup coconut vinegar
- cup sliced into wedges green cabbage
- 1/2 tsp. cayenne powder
- 1 cup sliced into wedges red cabbage
- 2 tbsp. olive oil
- 3/4 cup per person cooked white rice
- 1 tsp. brown sugar
- 1/2 cup grated carrots
- 1/8 tsp. roasted sesame oil
- 1 cup diced potatoes

Sauce:

- 2 tsp. cornstarch
- 2 tbsp. water

Method:

Step 1

Press the 'cook' button and put the machine on high setting.

Step 2

Heat the olive oil and then, sauté green and red cabbages until they are partially cooked.

Step 3

    Add cayenne powder, potatoes, water, brown sugar, red pepper flakes, coconut vinegar, and carrots. Cook for approximately 5 minutes.

Step 4

    Move to a platter.

Step 5

    At the same time, for the sauce, on the rice cooker press the "sauté" button.

Step 6

    Mix water and cornstarch. Cook mixture for approximately 4 minutes. Adjust to your liking.

Step 7

    Serve by placing an equal number of veggies. Pour the sauce on top of the vegetables. Use parsley to garnish. Enjoy.

29. Vegetable Chili and Zucchini

Serves: 4

Time: 30 mins.

The list of ingredients:

- 2 tbsp. plain flour
- A pinch of salt
- 2 tbsp. chili powder
- 1 can chopped tomatoes
- 1 cup sweetcorn

- 2 crushed garlic cloves
- A pinch of pepper
- 2 tbsp. tomato puree
- 1 large, wedges onion
- 1 red chunks bell pepper
- 1 ½ cups vegetable stock
- 1 tbsp. olive oil
- 1 large, chunks zucchini
- 1 can red kidney beans

Method:

Step 1

Press the button marked 'cook' on the rice cooker and heat the olive oil. Sauté onion for approximately 4 minutes.

Step 2

Add the garlic, bell peppers, zucchini, and the chili powder. Stir for around 4 minutes.

Step 3

Add in the flour then stir in the vegetable stock.

Step 4

Pour in the tomatoes (chopped) and tomato puree.

Step 5

Cook for roughly 10 minutes. Season using salt and pepper.

Step 6

Add in the sweetcorn and the kidney beans and let simmer for an additional 5 minutes. Serve.

30. Christmas Pumpkin and Red Bean Curry

Serves: 4

Time: 25 mins.

The list of ingredients:

- 2 tbsp. red curry paste
- 2 red chunked bell peppers
- 1 cup sugar snap peas
- 1 can aduki beans

- 2/3 cup vegetable stock
- 1 finely grated lemon grind
- 1 tbsp. soft, brown sugar
- 1 finely chopped onion
- 1 juice lemon
- handful coriander
- 2 green, thinly sliced chilies
- 1 cup baby leaf spinach
- 2 cups cubed pumpkin
- 1 ¼ cup coconut milk
- 2 tsp. minced ginger
- 1 tbsp. olive oil

Method:

Step 1

In a frying pan, begin to heat the olive oil and stir in the curry paste.

Step 2

Fry paste for roughly 1 minute then begin to add the chilies, onion, pumpkin, ginger, and bell peppers.

Step 3

Fry and stir for approximately 5 minutes then add the coconut milk and vegetable stock then bring to a boil.

Step 4

Tip mixture into the rice cooker and stir in the brown sugar, snap peas, lemon rind, aduki beans, and lemon juice. Cover rice cooker using the lid then cook for an additional 10 minutes.

Step 5

Toss in the coriander and spinach then serve immediately.

www.ingramcontent.com/pod-product-compliance
Lightning Source LLC
LaVergne TN
LVHW020825010225
802731LV00009B/646